This book is presented,
in celebration of Family, to

_____

by

_____

on

_____

Founded in 1869 as the publishing arm of The Lutheran
Church—Missouri Synod, Concordia Publishing House gives
all glory to God for the blessing of 150 years of opportunities
to provide resources that are faithful to the Holy Scriptures
and the Lutheran Confessions.

Published by Concordia Publishing House
3558 S. Jefferson Avenue, St. Louis, MO 63118–3968
1-800-325-3040 • cph.org

Manufactured in Shenzhen, China/022101/330251

1 2 3 4 5 6 7 8 9 10   28 27 26 25 24 23 22 21 20 19

God's Gift of Family

Written by Brenda Jank   Illustrated by Penny Weber

CONCORDIA PUBLISHING HOUSE • SAINT LOUIS

4

God made monkeys and mountains, moonlight and me —
and God is the Maker of our family.
It's all so amazing; we know it's just right.
God gave us each other to hug and hold tight.

Before you were born, we dreamed and we prayed
of how our family would come to be made.
We prayed for a child—just the right one—
who'd teach us to giggle and have lots of fun.

At just the right time,
in just the right way,
God gave you to us.
We shouted hooray!

You are a blessing. God calls you by name.

There's no one like you; no, not one is the same.

We took lots of pictures and gazed in your eyes.

You're the love of our lives and our favorite surprise.

Through your eyes of wonder, I love to see
the joyous new things that live around me . . .
like kittens and bubbles, rainbows and rocks.
We'll see the whole world as we go 'round the block.

In some things we're different,
in some things the same.
We like to show off
for our own hall of fame.

We learn from each other, we learn every day—
how to live, how to love,
how to work, rest, and pray.

We learn in a way that's uniquely our own.
We give it our best.
We are never alone.

17

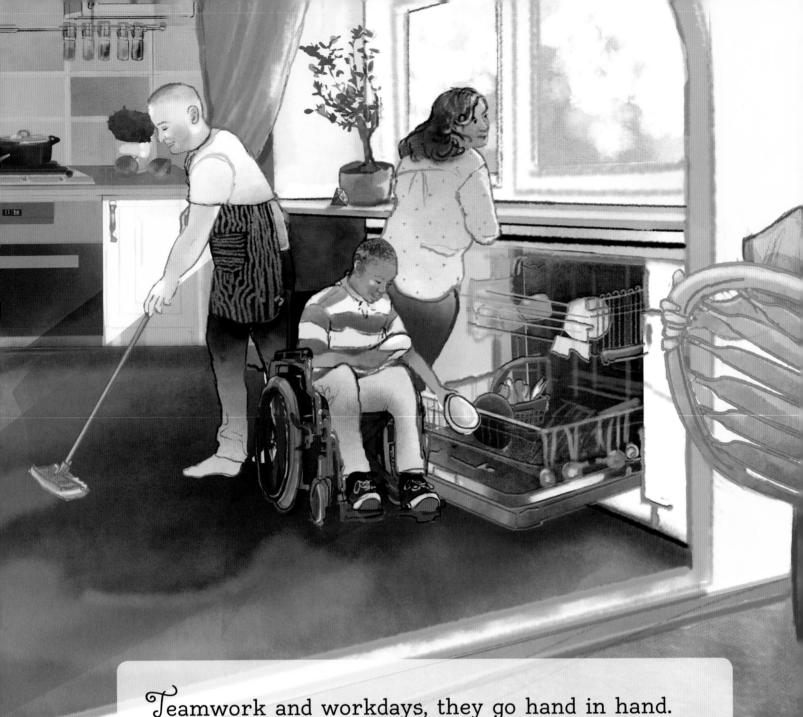

Teamwork and workdays, they go hand in hand.
We all work together. It's part of the plan.
We whistle and work, we scrub and we clean,
from ceiling to floor and all in between.

With lots of great planning and lots of great care,

God put us together to love, grow, and share.

Today we are happy, but sometimes we're sad.

And sometimes we might even get a bit mad.

Forgiving each other is part of God's plan.

God did it first so that we'd understand.

We are a blessing! God calls us by name.

There's nobody like us, no family the same.

We are a blessing! God made us just right.

He brought us together with joy and delight.

You are a blessing—we'll tell the world so!

We'll shout from the mountains and valleys below.

You are a blessing! We know it is true.

What a wonderful gift God gave us in you.

You are the finest—

God's perfect design.

I'll love you forever

and thank God you're mine.

God is the Maker of our family.

He did a great job. I bet you'd agree.

Glue a photograph of your family here.

GOD MADE OUR FAMILY